FROM LOVE...BACK TO LOVE

IS LOVE THE BEGINNING OR THE END?

**POEMS ON THE TIE THAT
BINDS, BREAKS AND BRINGS ONE BACK TO SELF**

TRINA D. ROBINSON

A VOICE IN WRITING, LLC

Published By
A Voice In Writing, LLC
10600 S. Pennsylvania Ave., Ste 16, PMB# 533
Oklahoma City, OK 73170
www.avoiceinwriting.com

From Love...Back To Love: Is Love The Beginning Or The End?

Paperback Edition ISBN: 978-1-7374674-3-4
eBook Edition ISBN: 978-1-7374674-2-7

Library of Congress Control Number: 2022910519

DEDICATION

I dedicate this book to all who were blindsided by love and lived to tell their story, leaving everything in between the pages and unafraid to love again.

FROM LOVE...BACK TO LOVE

IS LOVE THE BEGINNING OR THE END?

POEMS ON THE TIE THAT
BINDS, BREAKS AND BRINGS ONE BACK TO SELF

TABLE OF CONTENTS

THE BEGINNING

MOM AND DAD

What better way to look at love
Than through the lenses of my mother and father
Their time
When I was around
Was full of ups and downs
Mostly
Let downs that led to being picked up
Collecting these scenes in my memory
I see why I feel the need to query love's authenticity

It was three and a bonus one before me
Surely
Love did reside
In between bassinettes, matching black, blues and outfits
You would think
When I arrived
Bundled in pink
That would be the solution to everything
I always saw myself as a problem solver
A personalized sunbeam
Not even my dimpled face
Could replace the anger that permeated

Why did my mom stay
For y'all
She stated
Deep down I always speculated
It was to avoid the lonely
That dread that burrows in your head and lingers
Not to point fingers

Maybe my father's combative nature was for that same
reason
In some strange way
He fought to stay
On my mother's mind
On my mother's body

Eventually
Tough love made them part ways
They got the message
Hopefully
In seeking love
Their baby girl
Can rewrite the steps it takes

*I want someone to chase me.
I just don't feel like running.*

DON'T DISAPPOINT MOM

From grade school to high school
It was always head in the books, stay focused, make my
family proud and don't disappoint my mom
I did just that
Stuck to the script
No time for relationships
I had the life of my dreams that I needed to build

In junior high and high school
It seemed the pandemic was getting pregnant
I correlated boys with big bellies
Although I had responsibilities
No way was I ready for diapers, bottles and a baby
The girls who laid down dolls and picked up newborns
were all in love
Sadly enough
Their bundle of joy was the only reciprocation

After I entered into college
My focus didn't switch
I walked a tight rope between studying and dating
Swaying more toward the former rather the latter
Head in the books, focused, make my family proud and
don't disappoint my mom
When like ties ended, it didn't matter
Love was far from my mind
It helped that none of the guys were on my level
Or vice versa
The stares were few and far between from them
Then I saw him

What books
What focus
What family
Mom hush

I wanted to risk it all
He was the one
He was love
We had everything in common
Including our promised values
Head in the books, stay focused, make the family proud
and don't disappoint mom
Was his motto too

NEVER BEFORE

We never shared space
But I prefer you closer than apart
Instead of clothes or toys
You are the present I prayed my Father would present
You make my words sweeter with your essence
Every consonant, every vowel strategically placed
Like pieces to a jigsaw puzzle mysteriously revealing
your face
A bitter aftertaste erupts
When your expectations and I don't match up
I rewrite to catch up
Leaving multiple crumpled images of you surrounding
me
The only one who hugged away my breath and replaced
it with wanting
The only one who makes me smile while creating in the
pre-dawn hours of the morning
The only one who turns my dreams into nightmares
because I know when I wake you will be absent
My muse
Some accuse me of imaginative thinking
But I know never before
I don't think the same since we met
Who knew admiration could have this effect

*Just when I get a glimpse of this
mythical thing called love,
my focus changes.
Now, I'm torn between moving
forward with love and leaving
me behind.*

IT ALL STARTED AS A CRUSH

I had no business flirting with you
I didn't even know what I was doing
But I knew what I was doing
And it worked
I got your attention and your number
While we talk for hours
I wonder how
I'm different from the other girls you entertained
It doesn't matter
You're mine now
Such the gentleman
Opening doors
Pulling out my chair
No other couples could ever compare to our love affair
Gifts given just because they show how much we care
Forehead kisses for you
Gentle strokes of my hair
Never any bad energy or tension in the air
What should be a dream
Is our reality
I pray we stay the same
For eternity

I see myself in your eyes
You are a reflection of me
I'm not attracted to opposites
I need someone to be on my same wavelength
Someone I can be open with
Someone I can talk the world to
Without fearing judgment
You are that
Light to my confusion
The embodiment of my wishes and dreams
You are music
An instrument I'll never lay a hand on
I promise as many times as you need to hear it
You shine on your own without any interference
My compliment
I'm just words
You provide the beautiful melody
How it should be
How it always is

IN THE BEGINNING

A FRESH PIECE OF BUBBLEGUM

Let me sit this right here
Clean and pure
Untouched
Food for thought
Waiting for your key
Unlock my treasure's door
Adorn yourself with this long awaited warm welcoming

OUT OF CHARACTER

You killed me. I'm on my deathbed. While envisioning funeral arrangements, burial outfit, who I want to give my eulogy, I race my fingers down your spine and back up again.

Your fist is in my afro picking apart the tension whose safety of remaining intact I fought long and hard for. Tonight, I'm a sore loser. Tonight, my want to lose is one in comparison to my need for you. When I came too, I felt relief to be beside the machine I somehow knew would be above satisfactory.

However, I never suspected satisfaction stirring spirits surpassing that which we sipped subsequently staging me in a multiplication of staggering positions solidifying the tie between me and...and.... I screamed your government so much you'd think it would be committed to memory. That along with all other functions assigned to my brain you removed, screwed out like a light bulb—1,600 lumens, 1,600 strokes for the win.

Although I can think of synonyms, I don't remember what to call you. I bet the neighbors do. This is my something new, so out of character yet true. So out of character that the transformed womanly me agrees to let you snore in slumber a little longer, recharge to repeat. So out of character, but you're worth keeping.

YOUR MASTERPIECE

I'm that haunting image
Freed from your soul's captivity
A captivating beauty
Caramel skin tone
Similar to that which covers the apple
But not as soft or as sweet as my temple transcribed
from your memory
I'm that picturesque sunset
All aglow
The figurative pot of gold at the end of your troubled
rainbow
I'm the dots, the crosses, the scratch outs and
misspellings
That ink spot where the last of your emotions couldn't
wait to be released from within
The fading of words
From dark to light
The runoff from your weeping pen
I can be your greatest creation
Your heart on paper
Casted to become true
Or a faceless composition that's so compelling
Told to the world
But belonging only to you

Don't feel sorry for me.
If I'm drowning in love,
I'm drowning in love!

ART = LOVE = US

I'm intoxicated by paint fumes in the morning
Before my eyes flutter open
And I love it
Paint fumes means he's near
Painting away his frustrations and anxiety
Into a portrait of hope, elation, determination, tomorrow
And I love it
And I love him
And I love us

*He said I make him feel like a man.
I told him
forgive me for my failure.
It's my job to make him feel like a
King.*

THE ROYALTY I SEE EVEN IF HE DOESN'T BELIEVE

I used to think he was hard as cement
Undaunted
Unafraid of the monsters that lurked in imaginary caves
Poised in the face of fire breathing dragons
Strong enough to stand in for the centerpiece of a brick wall
Then I saw him fall
Realized his eyes could produce water
Grown man tears that salted his Earth with anger and anyone who walked on his ground
Deflated
After discovering not all things relinquish easily
But Kings are born not made
From the womb in tune with their purpose, promise and power
Birthed by a Queen
Therefore, I know the recipe to feed his foes
I know what settles his soul
I know the right words to use to form a canopy so those deep blues won't penetrate through
Let me cater you back to health
Not because I'm that type of submissive
It's my chosen position
To get you back to your former self

LET ME BE YOUR SOFT

let me restore you from the harsh weathering of the day
let me present you with tangible comfort
drop that tough guy performance in front of me
let me be the pillow you quietly scream into
let my digits get lost in your worries until I unearth that
grain of doubt and remove it
let me be the ocean waves that crash
on the land that doesn't want you to stand and be
the break you need
as I rock-a-by your psyche into peace
let me be calm in the face of your rage
patience in the wind of your uncertainty
life to your buried tomorrows
truth to their lies
hope to your regrets
strength
understanding
respect
love
soft

I get lost in things
to the point where
I can't recognize
start-up errors or the demise.

TALKING MESS

He got my gut going in circles
I go through bouts of hating him
To wanting to make another him
Or a mini me
Who would one day grow up and marry
A man that resembles the father that showered mommy
in love
Wish she never discovers
The current S-O-B
Sorry
His mother doesn't deserve the blame
It's not her fault her son's age is still the same
As when he suckled on her tits
She does coddle him and criticize me so maybe she's
not that innocent
A pinch
Is all the patience
I have left in this relationship
All the youth I wasted
Longing for a man who refuses to grow up and
welcomes being basic
I get so frustrated
I should've cheated
Wow, did I let that slip
Yes, I did and I meant it
But the lies he fed that kept him ranked highest priority
Those daydream tales etching
I love him
In my core
I ate up

Sure enough
It was all bullshit
Still
As I sit
Figuring out an escape route
Flashbacks of an affectionate him fogs my clarity
Verbal jabs and mental manipulation should be enough
to make me walk away permanently
Reluctantly
I'll wait
Until I formulate
A me-proof strategy for an actual eviction date
On the only throne I can claim that's made of porcelain
Venting and waiting for my man to come home
So I can be in love with him all over again.

I was a little too eager, a lot too unrealistic. Sometimes when you hear that clock ticking and see white gowns and tuxedos on your friends you tend to get that feeling of jumping the broom in and making right any wrong situation. I should've chose patience as a replacement for tying you to a proposal we weren't ready to engage in. Maybe that's what turned sour our sweet beginning. Our friends could see the house, the picket fence, which of our characteristics would display in our future kids but none of us could foresee our tumultuous ending. We started out one pod two peas. Whenever anyone saw you, they saw me. We placed each other in high regards of feelings and needs. Our love seemed unbreakable until the mention of taking it to the next level. Then, things changed and we sat on the opposite end of everything. Needs were neglected; however, feelings were still expressed in a meaningful way. In place of our usual love speech, I received your honesty debut of how you felt suffocated. I can't remember the last time we agreed. Our love faded. I don't even think time or common law would've saved it. It's the perception of perfection that did it. I made red flags rosy...

I ADMIT IT

REGIFTING

He asked how I could still have love for him after all
these years
That was the easiest question we ever exchanged
Because the nonsense, you never waded through
We were
Then we weren't
Throughout
I had my doubts
I wasn't the closest trigger to your side
When you confirmed
I soon learned
Some triggers shouldn't be internalized
Yet instilled
I was the prize
I want to see you do well though
Even if it's not with me
I genuinely want you to win
I saw the man you'd grow to be
Way back then
I knew you were special
A gift
Just not mine
To open

I used to love my lake portraits
I drank their purified water
Moistened my parched lips
Repeated my dips
Into swelled banks until I no longer wanted my thirst
momentarily quenched
Although love still flowed
Predictability provided a wedge
Leaving me with more sediments than sentiments
There's nothing wrong with variations of blues on
canvas
As long as it doesn't penetrate the soul
I'm opposed to stillness
Calm followed by the familiar, heart-breaking waves
With my common eyes closed
I crave
Vibrancy
No rules or boundaries
Free
From sanctioned mediums, sense, stationary position
Defying all laws and gravity
I've fallen for the strange, ornate, simple, chaotic beauty
My heart now only beats for

GRAFFITI

TEMPTATION

Refreshing
Breathtaking
Sincere
Considerate
Sexy
Intelligent
Stable
Confident
Strong
Comical
Humble
Driven
Sadly
Wanting
You
Back

I just found the letter that you wrote. I know this sounds like the beginning of an R&B love song but it just knocked me off my feet. I wasn't expecting to see it after all this time like I wasn't expecting to bump into you. Cold as ice was my heart, froze, the minute we fell through on our let's get married moment. I mean, our I dos. I'm not expressive in speech; however, I can put pen to paper and showcase my anger. You might be shocked to learn that those emotions I felt, I blame it on me. I begged for the shot to the heart; it was up to me to tackle the consequences after receiving. Instead, I tried blocking you out of my head. I pretended my love for you was dead as if things left unsaid would remain buried. All lies because how I truly felt remained alive and festered on the inside as a lost opportunity. How could I move on when every mannerism, every conversation, everything reminded me I wasn't in your presence? I got it bad, my bad, another musical reference. See, when you share I dos with someone you love, it's hard to pretend with some bodies that don't even matter. Nothing even matters. I'd never marry them. I also never want to make the same mistakes twice. So, if our chance meeting leads to a couple of forevers, there will be a meeting of the minds. An understanding that we are the only ones sharing each other's space and time. Time heals all ill wills. If willing, I'm willing for a vows renew. I miss you something terrible. I do, have love for you...

STILL

HIS EYES

He has fire in his eyes
Enough to engulf him and me both
I'm afraid
Nevertheless
I hold my breath at the stench of my burning flesh

LEAVING LOVE

I didn't want to depend on you anymore
I let you disarm me one too many times
I fell for your actions as a cure all
Instead of a stress reliever
You caused more headaches
Than my hardest worked days
I chose you to be a welcomed distraction
Not fun
But someone who could extract my burdens
And make me forget they existed
I would be the same for you
That ended quick
Instead of staying content
With your twin flame
You became inconsistent
Distracted by others fire work
I later uncovered where all my troubles travelled
On the cold side of the bed
Next to my tear soaked pillow
Love left its mark before it left me
Stuffing my car with moving boxes
Scrubbing soot to make sure I received my deposit
Change from the lessons gained
I could no longer live in the memories

MAN PLEAS

I cried so long and hard
But I knew what to do
I gave it to God
Then I felt the stress double
Like God gave it back
Because it was too superficial for Him to handle

I was insane to think of you as common and not rare
I never should've let you out of my grip
If I had you now
I'd ask you to marry me
Give you your first-born
For this to be
I know it will take a miracle

I'm willing to put in whatever work necessary
Truth is
It should've been this way initially
I allowed outsiders to intervene
I get it now
I'm determined to make our love everlasting

If there's someone in my place
Consider this their final notification
Getting you back is my primary concentration
Let me have a redo

Be honest from the start
Is what I'm going to do
The storms
We'll weather
From this day forward
Starts our forever

Who hadn't wanted that old thing back
 This time around
God himself told me I better not backtrack
He said I'd be better off putting those fantasies in a book
He told me He would send someone special
That I would know how to tell he was from Him
And to stop acting so hooked
When He knows I'm not listening
God keeps it real and speaks to me accordingly
I can't do anything but follow His instructions
But man…
Is so weak
I heed the words He speaks
Through thorough analysis
All that glittered wasn't gold
Nor meant to be

BUT MAN…

I crave your lips
Covering me with butter soft kisses
Allow the indentions of your smile to imitate fingertips
And interpret my body's twitches like Braille
With you is the only time I'm frail
Reflecting on our mouths last rendezvous
A ménage à trois of anatomy
How could I stay angry
How could I deny myself of you
Steak to this lioness
I would be lying
If I claimed I didn't hunger for your succulence
Can we indulge in each other again
You respond
Yes
In an instant
I'm back in your web
You waiting
Watching
For that familiar expression to come over my face
The expression of hunger
Ready to devour

FEED ME

It's a triumph
Against all oppositions
Light allowing new life to grow
Like a seed planted in March
Watered by April's tears from a broken heart
Only to survive and bloom
Becoming sturdier to withstand the heat of May, June
And beyond
July, August, September
Lies, Angst and Surrender
October, November
To the dead of winter
December
Remember

LET LOVE WIN

OUR SONG

We breathe
In and out
In sync
Which is why
I love you next to me
When we have to be away
The beat
Our song
Will forever play

It reminds me to carry on
The absence never lasts too long
Time quickly passes by
Escapes
I'm excited to be back in your embrace

Who ever thought I would find
Someone whose natural rhythm matches mine
It's no coincidence we're here
It's the music
Our own cadence
That will always draw you to me and me to you
My Dear

BEWARE OF TATTED LOVERS

I just wish the slate were wiped clean
I mean
To me you mean everything
But the stains from former flames constantly remind me
And I can't completely give in to
Can't completely be free to
Do those things that please you
Knowing your past is watching
Which is something I'm not into
Why did you get those tattoos
Especially the one in that spot
That one spot I know makes you
That spot that's my go to
Now compromised by some bygone thought
That used to cling to you
Make them move
Evict that ink
Like you did them
You know I'm much better
For this area
That when activated makes you rise out of your cool
Make you shout as if touched by spirits
Yeah that spot
You know it
That spot should be
Reserved for yours truly
I guess when the final straw drops
It will be
I'm starting to look at things differently
The images represent more than old romances

Conquer
Claim staked
Body count
Check mark
Notch
It's a reference to torment
Acquired from letting down your guard
Who caused you to be the way you are
Where did they leave you hurt
Point to the pain
Broken hardness
Turned to skin burns
Repossessed emotions
Reminder of never allowing another in
Instead of holding grudges to colorful names, faces and symbols
Masked suffering should be cause for concern

I was too "needy" so he pushed me away like I was hair in his face. As if I was ever that annoying.

MY NEEDS BEFORE YOUR WANT

I need commitment…
Love me and only me, openly and honestly

I need security…
Knowing all evil things seek their own safety when
you're around

I need to be inspired…
Show me greatness to complement and admire

I need brilliancy…
Scholarly and worldly intelligence to lead a household
and wisdom to know that your wife makes it a home

I need kindness…
When I'm at my lowest, you at your truest won't hold it
against me

I need tranquility…
Banning the chaos of the world from our personal
environment, if it's not nourishing it's not entering

I need attention…
Attend to me from my surface needs to anticipation

I need pouring into…
Mentally, spiritually, physically nurtured from the
bottom of my feet to the top of my head

I need respect...
If you don't want it done to you, don't do it to me

I need reciprocity...
As I give my all, give your all to me

I need love...

You want...
Me to be someone else

Nothing ever comes back the same, whether it's a borrowed item or affection. In terms of affection, it's our responsibility to make sure it comes back better.

BOOMERANG

I threw you a way
Out of a dead end situation
Then you threw me back
Paranoia and judgment
I gave you all that was in me
Even when you had enough
You didn't stop the flow
You just let me bleed
Coincidentally
My love flowed to someone who for me is more appropriate
Someone who sees me
Matches my interests
Our likes fit like magic
Abracadabra
You reappear
Out of fear
You lost the best you ever known
How sad
You had
On its own, the grass is never greener on the other side
It depends on the landscape artist and the light they provide
You were more like an escape artist who closed your eyes on me causing your own light to dim
They use their light to magnify mine within
We're planting roots, growing stronger, healthier
I'm much happier with my own wakeup call not just the presence of them
Love at last swung in my direction
You can swing back to whom or wherever

CHECKLIST

<u>HIM</u>
Sexy
Beautiful Smile
Hypnotizing Eyes
Charming
Hustler
Accomplished
Flashy
Poor Communicator
Not Dependable
Not Trustworthy
Liar
Liar
LIAR
Insecure
Manipulator
Narcissist
Unstable
Toxic
Toxic
TOXIC

<u>ME</u>
CRAZY
For wanting him back

DÉJÀ VU

Where do we go from here?

I've internalized the last of my tears.

It's time I split myself open and give my insides a
chance to dry.

I can't change my misfortunes, but I can forfeit that bad
luck from carrying over to my future emotions.

Time matures you.

With these wise eyes as truth detectors, even though my
flesh wants to reconnect my spirit is more complex
demanding me to show the Queen within some respect
and because of that, I can see right through you.

I put you on a pedestal.

For lack of a better metaphor, you were the hungry
plant, and I Seymour, who I fed my time and energy to
thinking I would see more of you only to not place
because your priorities took up that space.

I did move on.

Just as I started to become strong on my own, distraction
comes along with you in its grasp and I gave in too fast
when the nostalgic memories that whispered in my ear
should've stayed in the past.

Where do we go from here?

I put you on a pedestal.

With these wise eyes as truth detectors, even though my flesh wants to reconnect my spirit is more complex demanding me to show the Queen within some respect and because of that, I can see right through you.

Time matures you.

I can't change my misfortunes, but I can forfeit that bad luck from carrying over to my future emotions.

It's time I split myself open and give my insides a chance to dry.

I've internalized the last of my tears.

Where do we go from here?

TECHNICAL MALFUNCTION

With every tear, the byproduct of my misery, embedded into the threads of my clothes like cheat codes for self-destruction, I stayed. Stood there and smiled as all the downloaded files of lies and deceit played. I stayed as if to ask for more, more bullshit, more avoidance, more less you. The one I loved. The only one whose love I wanted. In seeking your acceptance, I destroyed me. You corroded my mind frame, ripped out my heart's drive and reprogrammed it all for you, none for me. I need my sanity restored. I'm not the toy of a bored boy. I'm a woman who deserves to love unconditionally and not be held captive for doing so until you realize I was the one you needed all along. You being you said no.
So, I turned those slow crawling shards reserved for you into fuel. In order to reboot, I had to let myself go.

WHAT IF

What if I chose You instead of love?

I picked what I believed was the path less travelled.
It was too late when I noticed the sod was Astroturf and
underneath tracks for miles.
Regretting decisions I made was never my style.
Besides, I had intuition on my side,
That gut feeling that never steered me wrong.
Plus, I knew love came with storms.
It's just a rough patch.
Give it time,
It'll pass.
That's what I told myself over the years.
Over the years, the rough patches recycled and the sky
was nowhere near clear.

What if I challenged it?
What if instead of settling for love I said I quit?
Put me back on the bench.
The games I had to play just to get love's
acknowledgement wasn't worth it.

What if I chose You instead of love?

Would the worries and drama be less?
Would there be any stress?
What if this was all a test
To attest
I didn't know what was best?

THE ENDING

AND THEN MY CRUSH CRUSHED ME

It all stopped unexpectedly
No phone calls, no texts back
No need to check socials
I was blocked on all of that
What did I do wrong
Was my love that strong to reverse yours to hate
I never tried to hide my eccentric nature
Nor my shortcomings
Mask on
When you first said you loved me
Those traits you didn't see
Mask off
Now that we're not living in bliss
My inadequacies are all you bring up to me
The buildup of remarks about my body parts
Unanswered requests for conversations covering
concerns
Constructed walls that no matter how hard I worked out
of love they're not coming down
Bridge burned
Perhaps it's someone else's turn
To love me without terms
It may be
Someone else's turn

MUSIC THERAPY

Broken promises brought me here
I need the rhythm to beat strength into me
Lyrics, like light, highlight likenesses to my real life
On the bed
Sprawled out on my back
Unable to sit upright
Myself, me, I, alone
Looking at the ceiling
While reminiscing
Fan blades mimicking the rotation of my vinyl record
Player was his hidden profession
Got me drowning my sorrows in the same manner we
welcomed in tomorrows
From baby making music to the subdue crazy tunes
Created eras before I was even considered being born
Rebel rousing spiritual rebirth songs
Taking away all the vulnerability
Blues turning my blues into happy
Cool jazz icing my veins
I've already forgotten our heated exchange
Payback music circling back to love ballads provides
solace
With my eyes watching my eyelids
I prepare for a mental disappearance

*When you've reached
the eye of a storm, you can't help
but look disheveled.*

I'm a mess
Hair unkept
Wrinkles in my shirt
Jeans on their third day of unwashed wear
Shoes, slip on, the most comfortable I own
My friends and family ask
What's wrong
Even though they saw this me before and already knew
I held on to love too long
Got caught up in the whirlwind
Now that it ended
I'm unsure how to carry myself

ALONE

WHEN YOU'RE BROKEN AND DON'T KNOW IT

I was losing water
Tears from my eyes
First at a slow pace
Then when I realized I walked into the same mistake
It was as if someone opened the floodgates
We are mostly water beings
A drop I couldn't afford to dissipate
In being a human being I can't help but utilize these
windows to the soul as my method of releasing
However
I stay stuck in the same old feelings
It's intriguing
While inquiring

Have you ever felt unappreciated?

*Have you ever had to decide whether to stay or deal
with the suffering of moving on?*

*Does the other side of your bed ever stay cold for too
long?*

You're not responding
How silly of me
To be so conceited
Thinking I was your answer
Everything you needed
That voice in my head even cried and pleaded

Stay away!

It ain't him!

He's not the one!

Nevertheless
I told myself
I could win the game
My strategy I didn't abort
We were on different skill levels
Me a beginner
You an advance professional
No wonder I got scorched
Broken
Temporary acts of benevolence
Repaired me for return visits
When will I learn real love
And know that you are not it

PROPERTY OF ME

Find your name on me
You left it there
When you left me there
Staring at you slip out as the sun slipped in
Still yours
Just waiting for you to claim
The games you played
Should've said a thousand goodbyes
Every time I see your face
Old feelings of loneliness make room for young ones
It's because you left something behind
When you gather your brand
That turns push-away to come here baby
Then I'll be fine
Is what I tell my heart every time
Yet here we are
Doing the only thing we do best
Come
It won't be hard to locate
You were the only one
This heartache is yours to alleviate
Find your name on me
I'm not like you
I don't take possession of something I don't want to
belong to
I need to regain time wasted
Take back my dignity
Remove your name so I can stand
As my own property.

*I tossed plenty of pennies in wells
wishing for love.
No wonder my returns were so low.*

I WISH

I wish you were the person you pretended to be. That's it, that's the wish. You were terrible at keeping up the facade anyway. You'd be better off working harder on you to turn the illusion into truth. I guess that sounds too much like right and you were all wrong.

You can pray all you want.
You can hope all you want
but if the other person isn't
on the same page,
nothing's going to change.

Pray for you. Pray for someone
better for you. Pray for the living
because you know the
relationship is dead.

NO MORE PRAYERS FOR THE DEAD

I prayed for our survival
I prayed for us to match up united not as rivals
I prayed for harmony
I prayed for all the lies to cease
But if you're not in it
Right here by my side
What point is it to fight for relief

You tell me you love me
You say it with no coercion
Then I uncover signs
I can no longer act blind
How could you betray me

I prayed for you to see
All that you mean to me
I prayed that I could be
Half of that to you at least

All you gave
Was a shaking head
Saying
No
When I know your no means
Yes

Now I pray for self-value
I pray not to cause harm to you
I pray for no more clues
It hurts when I know the truth

I pray for my recovery
I pray for courage to move on from you
I pray for my intuition to improve
So a connection as wrong as us
I will never again go through

I pray for sunny days
Someone else to embrace
Someone willing and able to love
A representation of Your grace

TEARS TO REMEMBER

If I'm crying
That means I'm attached
Holding on to some slim chance
You have me in the palm of your hand
I want all my tears back
I'll travel the rest of my days with buckets
Use the water to grow blooms of hope
Not weeds of reluctance
Perhaps I'll baptize myself
Reclaim my time along with the remnants of memories
Souvenirs to remember the agony
Of giving all of me to someone else

WE USED LOVE WRONG

Love's definition is an intense feeling of deep affection.

I faddishly turned it into an exclamation mark to express how deep you penetrated my thoughts. I know actions are greater than expressions. By my logic, if you heard me say, "I love you" repeatedly, even I would believe. Not that I didn't have strong feelings. I'm just left seeking the one who makes me feel seen and my soul smile, someone capable of answering who and what accompanied with they are and they need respectively.

You misused love also. You treated it as a placeholder, pausing Option B in case Option A didn't go as expected and you had the alternate to revolve back to. It's likely you enjoyed my company but loving me was a different story. I'm too forward to be a backup plan. Either accept all and only what I have to offer or don't bother disrupting my serenity.

CALL ME STUPID

Even when I had you in
My heart
My everyday routine
I didn't have you into me
Respectfully
Seriously
How stupid was I to think
I had the ability to match casual with wedding gown
How stupid was I to think
Prayer would force you to come around
How stupid was I to think
I would be the one to foster your life cycle
To grownup from immaturity
How stupid was I to think
How stupid was I
How Stupid

I know he's not having sleepless nights.
He's not sitting home alone wondering what he could've done differently.
I know he's not shedding tears…please.
So why should I?
I should be more like him...

UNBOTHERED

I removed love's blinders.
For the last time, the
decision to part hit and stuck.

CHANGE IS INEVITABLE

You and I are like oil and water
We don't mix
Took a while for me to get
I'll never forget
I'm packing all your stuff in cardboard boxes
Pick them up in three days
No contact
No show
They're out the door
I won't bleach or blaze
Undoubtedly
Fashion is your most decent quality
They can go to the less fortunate
The only thing I'm burning is sage
To rid the air of broken commitment
And the resentment for the insolence I forgave
I'm not dwelling on the foolishness
Don't get me wrong
The optics of being power couple goals was cute
But I have a handle on realism
And can carry my dreams on my own
The plans and conquering will come true
Without you

Sometimes we have to settle for
It's not you, it's me.
Sometimes the
It's just not meant to be.
Is the only resolution we should seek
To see them move on so effortlessly
As if we never existed
Like we didn't have a whole chest of drawers
Half the closet
Like throughout the house and on the linens
Our scent didn't linger
Is sufficient enough
To wipe clean their memory
Like a steam covered mirror
Look at yourself and believe
The silence received
When all we wanted to do was clear the air so we could
settle in peace
Is relief
To not hearing any more lies that flowed naturally
I can say this
That false bliss won't be missed
When we know true love does exist
It will have no trouble finding us
Once we remove all one-sided compromises
The last reaction from us they need

BOWING OUT GRACEFULLY

LEAVING LOVE AGAIN

It's different this time
My eyes dry
My heart light
My attitude upbeat
My body calm
I knew the moment would come
Women like me
Eventually
Breakaway from men like you
The ones with greedy appetites and plenty of options
You weren't changing
I had to show accountability
By resigning from your open door philosophy
I'm breathing clean oxygen
A revival
With all the chosen baggage I can carry
Plus the slight smear of mustered up stamina
My life resets

YESTERDAY

I walked out
Left drama behind
The choice was mine
I chose mending
Not depending
On old feelings

TODAY

I woke up stronger
Prisoner no longer
Yawned to release held breaths anticipating right
decision-making that never saw daylight
Finally able to lay the past down without a fight
No more fairytale fantasies
My real life is better than any hopeless romantic movie

PEACE

My gift for both of us
I concluded
I reached maximum care capacity
I'm walking in faith through opened doors
Metaphors for better opportunities
Blessings received
Solo
I'm releasing your dead weight
Since the only thing you wanted to cling to was my
coattail believing that would get you in the same
doorways
I recognize I'm on another level and different journey
One you're not meant to follow
Calmness
Still
Goodbye
Is all I have left to offer you

REWRITING MY STORY

I'm the orchestrator of all this anguish
I forgot to end my nightly vent journaling with
Never again, Amen!
A proclamation
In not doing so
I walked right into the same stalemate
Relationships crashed and sunk like the Titanic on a loop
Repetition kills common sense
I'll never write that way again

THE COUNSEL IN RECONCILIATION

DON'T DO IT
DON'T DO IT
DON'T DO IT
THEY HAVEN'T CHANGED
THEY WILL NEVER CHANGE
THIS IS WHO THEY ARE
BELIEVE THEM
DON'T DO IT
DON'T DO IT
DON'T DO IT
YOU DESERVE BETTER
YOU WILL RECEIVE BETTER
STOP LIVING IN THE PAST
SAME PERSON WILL YIELD THE SAME RESULTS
MOVE ON
DON'T LOOK BACK
DON'T GO BACK
PROTECT YOUR PEACE
PROTECT YOUR ENERGY
PROTECT WHAT YOU ESTABLISHED
LET GO
LET GO
LET GO

I wanted him before any of my needs. He knew it, but I don't think he believed. I would've gone through great lengths to show it was true. Fortunately, it was something I never got the chance to prove.

THANK YOU

You did it on purpose, used my love for you as a tether. Kept me bound and close with allusions of together forever. You knew you didn't own genuine qualities necessary to maintain an unrestricted hold on me. The spell you casted was no match for the protection I'm covered in. You assumed your branded effects in my epidermis would make it harder for the next one who surfaces. Not true. You thought you blocked me from finding someone superior. You only made it impossible for me to find another you.

FIXED

I was your wife.
Who knew you had a harem?
I was your one and only, your rock, at least that's the lie
you sold to me.

Why didn't I do my research?
Before I allowed myself to fall in lust mislabeled,
I wished I conversed with the streets that owned you.

The only strong foundation laid down was...
Never mind,
Never wholly mine
Though.
I was a willing giver.
You were my addiction.
With any first fix,
You chase that high for the rest of your life but none
afterward would ever compete.

Lucky for me,
I never reached the point of cutting the satisfaction of
flesh with disrespect of my body.
I realized I needed much more than an unrelenting
receiver.
I quit you cold turkey.
I worked on my issues, decided not to participate in any
other weddings.
The only fix I needed was self-discipline.

He made me turn to crystal.
Not meth,
but the methodology of holding polished stones with
healing properties instead of him,
the server of all my heart's pain.
I feel God looking down at me in shame.
Sternly saying, "I told you, I close doors for a reason.
This was your season for prosperity,
you wanted to live in the past.
Welp, let this misery settle on your stuck on stupid-"
As I ask for forgiveness and mercy,
He said, "Just return your focus on me."

NOT A MAN...AMEN

NOTHING MORE, NOTHING LESS

My reservoir of happiness
The wisdom of all things
The peace that keeps me sane
Conqueror of my pain
The calm that settles my storms
The storm that shakes my complacency
Eraser of my fears
Deliverer of all chased dreams
The One who gave His life for me
Wanting nothing more than exaltation
And I give Him nothing less

What do you do when you have an abundance of unconditional love, support and comfort to give to someone who doesn't exist?

You keep it for yourself.

SELF-ISH

Self-taught
Self-learned
Self-absorbed
Self-defeated
Self-destroyed
Self-built

One time

Self-destroyed
Self-built

Two times

Self-destroyed
Self-built

As many times as necessary

Until I'm
Self-healed
Self-confident
Self-determined
Self-aware
Self-reflecting
Self-respecting
Self-removed
From that which no longer serves my purpose
To thy self be true showing that I'm
Self-approved
Self-motivated

Self-centered
In how I carry myself
Self-ish
With whom I choose to give my energy to
Self-ish
In how I spend my time
Self-ish
In the fact that before I can love anyone else
I must know

Self-love

TEARS DON'T KISS MY CHEEKS ANYMORE

I cried and cried
Because on the outside
I was weak

My body knew
My soul knew
What I possessed within was offended

I came from a long line of survivors
Not criers
Hard fought warriors of liberation
Their legacy for goodness sake
Was at stake

The epitome of those who carry on
The epitome of generations who with time got stronger
I'm not crying over minuscule matters any longer

My lineage has overcome
Far worse than love's burn
Lessons learned
Make up the essence of me
Recovering from love's sting
Led to me existing

I'm not allowing
Tears from love's hurt
Dive from the lashes of my eyes

Kiss my cheeks

RENEWAL

Walking in the rain
Letting the drops wash away
All the blemishes

I will never be
The same person you knew then
Love made sure of that

I welcome the downpours
The drought
The snow and ice
Those claustrophobic days when I don't receive time out
Because I know whether good or bad
Whether make me unrecognizable or have my
imperfections showing
I'm still growing

Love seems to follow the petals
We must acknowledge the roots
Stemming from constant changes
Whether unwarranted or pursued
Manifesting into our undeniable truth

Just because we were cultivated in a field of tragedy
Torn down
Plucked out
Picked apart
We can overcome and in turn discover our distinctive
beauty

So whether through the wettest of storms
Or the driest of circumstances
All of us
Roses
Wildflowers
Vines
Weeds

Must continue to
Keep blooming
Keep blooming

KEEP BLOOMING

WYD

What am I doing?
What do you think?
You tried to dilute my character
Not knowing I'm a bounce backer.
Still,
Your failure to love properly doesn't fare well.
I feel like that character in that movie,
"Until you do…"
Then I see the picture is bigger than just me.
You need to atone for all the women you did wrong,
Those who fell for lies disguised by your alluring eyes.
The windows to the soul,
Surprise,
I didn't realize how cold and dead you are inside.
Not a care for anything in the world,
Not even yourself.
The manipulating,
The cheating,
Your MO,
The poison you were dealing,
Only rotting your vessel,
Contaminating the carrier;
Meanwhile,
Your survivors are healing.
As for me,
I'm thriving
Wonderfully well without you…
Shining!
Thanks for asking.

You were my ending and the catalyst for my new beginning. I fell out of love with you and deeper in love with me.

FROM LOVE…BACK TO LOVE

Hey Love
It's been a minute
I'm tapped back in
Transformed
From tribulations
To loving someone deserving

Me

It's hard to believe
I didn't believe
I was worthy
Built up the wrong buildings
Sought approval in the wrong beings
Overstayed in their company
When I tried to seek more
It became a repetitive routine
Didn't think You were listening
I desperately wanted better
And knew it was possible
Better was just a mirror meeting away

Hello Beautiful

Brighter days are ahead
Worst days are in the rearview

Never again, Amen!

CALL TO ACTION

I need your help to spread the word about *From Love...*
Back To Love: Is Love The Beginning Or The End?

1. If you have a website or blog, share how the book touched you. Don't give away the plot, but recommend that they read it and then link to **avoiceinwriting.com**.
2. Write a review for your local paper, favorite magazine, website and/or Amazon.com.
3. Ask your favorite radio show/news outlet to have **Trina D. Robinson** as a guest. Media people often consider the requests of their listeners/viewers.
4. Talk about the book on email lists, forums and social networking sites. Don't make it an advertisement, but rather share how this book affected your life and offer a link to the site.
5. Stay Connected! Sign-up at **avoiceinwriting.com** to receive the newsletter, blog posts and get information on new releases, events, etc. Please follow **Trina D. Robinson** and **A Voice In Writing, LLC** on Facebook and Instagram. Also, subscribe to my YouTube channel, **A Voice In Writing**.

www.avoiceinwriting.com
FB & IG: @avoiceinwriting
FB & IG: @TrinaDRobinsonTheAuthor
YouTube: @avoiceinwriting